Minoans

A Captivating Guide to an Essential Bronze Age Society in Ancient Greece Called the Minoan Civilization

Free Bonus from Captivating History (Available for a Limited time)

Hi History Lovers!

Now you have a chance to join our exclusive history list so you can get your first history ebook for free as well as discounts and a potential to get more history books for free! Simply visit the link below to join.

Captivatinghistory.com/ebook

Also, make sure to follow us on Facebook, Twitter and Youtube by searching for Captivating History.

Contents

Introduction

The Minoans continue to be an intriguing subject for modern audiences because they are like a puzzle missing half of its pieces. Individuals have a rough idea of what it might look like, but there could be surprises no one even thinks of because all traces of the image are gone. For archaeologists, historians, tourists, scholars, fans of mythology, and students of the ancient world, the Minoans are this broken puzzle.

The Minoans were an ancient civilization that built their settlements on islands in the Aegean Sea. They lived almost 5,000 years ago and left behind traces of their lives but not enough for people to create a complete picture. Ever since the early 20th century, the Minoans have been a subject of interest thanks to the discoveries and excavations by Sir Arthur Evans, a British archaeologist who found the first Minoan ruins and named them after the mythological King Minos and his Minotaur. Evans was able to gain almost sole access to the lands of the Cretan government for excavation by paying for it with funds generated by his supporters in 1900. He and his crew unearthed the massive palace complex of Knossos, one of the most famous archaeological excavation sites in history.[1]

From the work of Evans and others, the puzzle of the Minoans has slowly gained more pieces. Through the study of material culture, modern audiences now know quite a bit about artistic techniques, favorite subjects, fashion, daily life, gender roles, and who the Minoans traded with. An observer can tell that the Minoans were a seafaring mercantile civilization, that they built magnificent urban centers, and that they had a form of proto-writing. However, much remains a mystery. We, as a global culture, have almost no idea about Minoan history.

Who were their enemies?

Did they war with their neighbors?

Did they have great monarchs and nobles?

Who was the snake goddess in their sculptures?

Did they really practice human sacrifice?

Were women the true leaders of religion?

What on earth was bull-leaping?

Perhaps most importantly: Which catastrophes weakened the civilization enough that they were overrun by their militaristic neighbors on mainland Greece?

This volume is less of a history and more of an interpretation and description of archaeological findings based on the testimonies and research of hundreds of scholars in the field. Based on the information contained herein, what do you, the reader, think the Minoans were like?

---

[1] Rodney Castledon, *Minoans: Life in Bronze Age Crete*, Routledge: Philadelphia, 1993.

Chapter 1 – Where and When Did the Minoans Live?

The Minoans were one of the Aegean Bronze Age civilizations that lived on islands like Crete and other landmasses on the Aegean Sea. They were a seafaring people who built their settlements on a series of small islands near modern-day Greece, and evidence indicates they traveled across the entirety of the Mediterranean Sea to trade with nearby cultures. The Minoans lived from c. 2700 BCE–c. 1100 BCE. When it comes to years, the designation BCE stands for Before Common Era, or before the contemporary year 1 in the modern Gregorian calendar. The Minoans would have therefore lived almost 5,000 years ago.

The World of the Minoans

The Bronze Age was a period in human development where civilizations were capable of creating bronze weapons and tools. Other requirements to be considered a Bronze Age civilization were possessing some form of proto-writing as well as urban civilization. To create bronze, the Minoans would have been able to smelt copper and alloy with other metals like tin and components like arsenic. The Minoans were actually one of the first people to master the ability to not only create bronze but also trade it with other civilizations that were unable to mine the necessary materials.

According to ancient Greek historians, the Minoans supposedly built 90 settlements on the island of Crete and numerous towns on the small islands nearby. Archaeologists have found concrete evidence of Minoan civilization only on Crete and a nearby cluster of islands originally called Thera, now known as Santorini. Crete is, by far, the most significant of the two areas because the majority of surviving Minoan artifacts have been found at large sites like Knossos, which archaeologists believe was the capital of Minoan civilization.[2]

---

[2] Ibid.

Although small, there is evidence indicating the population of Knossos grew rapidly and attracted the Minoan social and cultural elite. Estimates state that the city's population was 1,300 to 2,000 in 2500 BCE, 18,000 in 2000 BCE, 20,000 to 100,000 in 1600 BCE, and 30,000 in 1360 BCE.

Numerous artifacts come from Minoan palace structures which managed to survive the Mediterranean climate, attacks by enemies, and even a tsunami that devastated parts of Crete during the Late Minoan Age. Palaces tended to be massive stone structures with multiple rooms for storage, recordkeeping, and habitation. Other important sites for information and artifacts are caves where objects from ritualistic cult worship have been uncovered, as well as hamlets that contained pottery fragments. Some of the most significant locations for Minoan information, besides Knossos, are Phaistos, Agia Triada, Vasiliki, Arkalochori, and Akrotiri.

Some of the people the Minoans traded and interacted with were the Egyptians, the civilizations on mainland Greece, the societies of the Levant, and potentially eastern European civilizations in places like contemporary Romania. Many Minoans spent their life on the sea, traveling, fishing, and trading. Unlike other ancient civilizations, the Minoans had no need for a large standing army because they were surrounded by water on all sides and there weren't many powerful navies in the region. Instead, the Minoans stayed safe by shoring up their vessels and warding off pirates.

Excavations

A big problem when studying a civilization as ancient as the Minoans is that records were scarce and what did exist has suffered thousands of years of erosion and devastation. The Minoans, in particular, were a small group that did not keep many records, and while they did have the proto-writing system of Linear A, the existing documents are currently untranslated and unintelligible. Even worse, their homeland islands were hit by several disasters, including a massive volcanic eruption and a tsunami, as well as the conquest by their neighbors on mainland Greece, the Mycenaeans.

To obtain information about the civilization, archaeologists and other professionals excavate significant sites to find artifacts and preserved information. They then need to use logic and evidence to piece together who the Minoans might have been, how they lived, and their general social structure. Although there are currently dozens of different excavation sites throughout the Aegean and Mediterranean Seas, the most important are on Crete and Santorini, which is called Thera, the name found in ancient records from the Mycenaeans and Ancient Greeks.

From these sites, archaeologists, historians, and other scholars have managed to piece together a cohesive picture of the Minoans, although large gaps in knowledge still remain.

Chapter 2 – Known History of the Minoans before the Mycenaeans

The Minoans were an ancient civilization that stretched back thousands of years if one considers the original humans that settled on Crete. Humans have been living in and around the Mediterranean Sea for over 130,000 years, which is when scientists speculate that the first hominins arrived at places like Crete. The first modern humans are believed to have evolved around 10,000 BCE or 12,000 BCE based on archaeological evidence like stone tools, pottery, and skeletons discovered around the island. This evidence supports the idea that the Minoans and the Greeks shared common ancestors that originated in Anatolia or the Levant.

Because a Minoan civilization existed for centuries, historians and others tend to divide the years into three separate periods: The Early Minoans (MMI), the Middle Minoans (MMII), and the Late Minoans (MMIII). Despite having numerous examples of material culture from each period, little is known about the civilization's actual history. As mentioned, the people did not keep detailed records and did not often engage in wars, so major events are a mystery. Even the names of kings and nobles are difficult to come by, although there is adequate evidence to suggest disparate economic classes.

So, instead of details, historians are able to craft rough approximations of what developments occurred during each period. These are what are listed here.

The Early Minoans (MMI)

The first vestiges of Minoan civilization developed around the Early Bronze Age, which lasted from 3500 BCE to 100 BCE. Numerous authors indicated this time demonstrated the potential promises of the future Minoan civilization, which managed to thrive with little warfare. Evidence indicates that the hominins first started to form urban centers around the late 3000s BCE and then gradually developed recognizable Minoan civilization. These centers tended to be along the coastline and were locations where the elites could flock to engage in commerce and prepare a rudimentary social structure. Early Minoan life was characterized by the rise of monarchies. The monarchs displaced local elites who were more akin to tribal leaders, individuals influential in their own small communities that probably experienced some form of popular election. The first Minoan palaces date to this period.

The Middle Period (MMII)

Middle Minoan life continued much the same as it had for the Early Minoans. The population grew exponentially, and there is some evidence for technological and artistic developments that made it easier for traders to cross the Aegean and Mediterranean Seas. The Middle Minoan period lasted from roughly 2100 BCE to 1600 BCE. Something big happened toward the end of this period which resulted in a massive disturbance and widespread destruction on Crete. Palaces across the island were destroyed, including Phaistos, Knossos, Malia, and Kato Zakros. Archaeologists and historians believe the disruption was caused by a massive earthquake, potentially from the nearby volcanoes. There is also some speculation that the Minoans suffered an invasion from nearby Anatolia, but little evidence of armed combat remains.

During this period, the Minoan population declined and remained low for several decades. Toward the end of the Middle Period, the population once again saw an increase. Between the 17th and 16th centuries BCE, archaeologists think the Minoans entered their golden age, or the apex of civilization. This would have been a time when the culture and economy thrived and where the Minoans were at the height of their trading capabilities with other civilizations. Examples of material culture, or objects like pottery and jewelry, were found in high numbers on the Greek mainland. This meant the Minoans were producing more goods and significant demand for them existed in other places.

The Late Minoans (MMIII)

Around 1600 BCE, the Minoans suffered another devastating catastrophe, this time the eruption of the volcano in Thera. Although the eruption itself was not far-reaching, the force generated by the underground explosion created a massive tsunami that struck other islands, including Crete. Much of the Minoan architecture was destroyed, and settlements struggled to rebuild. The Minoans had to reconstruct several of their palaces, which resulted in different functions.[3] They were less about beauty and more used for sheer practicality.

However, they didn't last. In 1450 BCE, there's evidence the Minoans struggled with the aftermath of another natural disaster, most likely an earthquake. Multiple palaces were destroyed, including those at the settlements of Malia and Phaistos. Although the palace of Knossos remained largely intact, the living quarters and personal chambers did not. Scientists believe the earthquake was the

---

[3] John C. McEnro, *Architecture of Minoan Crete: Constructing Identity in the Aegean Bronze Age*, University of Texas Press, 2010.

result of another eruption at Thera, and historians think the earthquake was instrumental in the downfall of the Minoans.

Why though is mostly a mystery. The safety of the palace of Knossos meant the Minoans still had their center of culture and trade, so they were able to continue to influence other regions in the Aegean and Mediterranean Seas. They were, however, severely weakened. Scholars believe this weakness led to the Minoans eventually being overrun by the Mycenaeans on mainland Greece.

The decline during the period of the Late Minoans was therefore slow yet steady until the conquest of the Mycenaeans. Sometime around the 13th century BCE, the cities and palaces throughout the Aegean started to decline and lose their influence and population. Linear A, the Minoan writing system, started to disappear. By 1200 BCE, even Knossos lost its power as an administrative center.

What Happened?

There is little-known history about the Minoans, so it's almost impossible to ascertain the civilization's story. Historians and archaeologists do not know the names of influential nobles or kings, whether there were any significant battles, or even the ups and downs of daily life. The limited history of the Minoans does point to one potential avenue though: the Mycenaeans.

As far as scholars can tell, the Minoans most likely disappeared because a series of natural disasters left their civilization weak. This weakness led the Mycenaeans, who lived nearby on mainland Greece, to invade and take over important cultural and administrative centers. The presence of the Mycenaean writing system and artifacts in Minoan cities, dating to after the time of the Minoans, indicates the Mycenaeans most likely moved in and took over.

This strange enemy of the Minoans actually was not that different. The Mycenaeans as a people shared many of their roots with the Minoans and actually engaged in similar behaviors, relying heavily on trade to make ends meet. Some of the main differences were in military and religion. The Mycenaeans needed to possess a strong military since they lived on the mainland, and the culture prized military prowess and abilities more than the Minoans. The Mycenaeans were also the precursor to ancient Greek religion, developing the predecessors of famous gods and beliefs.

Who Were the Mycenaeans?

The Mycenaean Greeks, also called the Mycenaeans, were the last group in the Aegean Sea that belonged to the Bronze Age. They rose to power around 1600 BCE and lasted until 1100 BCE, creating a civilization that lasted for over 500 years. The people developed numerous urban organizations, created beautiful works of art, and possessed a writing system that historians understand which could have been used for recordkeeping and messages. The primary centers of power for the Mycenaeans were Athens, Midea, and Mycenae. Mycenae could have been considered the capital and was located in the Argolid and hosted the most influential nobles and greatest examples of culture. Outside of mainland Greece, the Mycenaeans developed settlements in Macedonia, the Levant, and Italy.[4]

The Mycenaeans would fall during the Bronze Age Collapse, which was when the Bronze Age civilizations throughout Europe, Asia, and Africa simultaneously crumbled. The exact causes are unknown, with theories ranging from sudden natural disasters to the invasion of the Sea Peoples, a strange group referred to in several documents that no one is sure about. When the Mycenaeans fell, they took with them some of their great advancements and pushed the Aegeans into the Greek Dark Age. Their successors would be the ancient Greeks, perhaps the most famous civilization known to Western audiences.

Since so much Minoan history is an empty canvas, historians haven't pieced together whether the Minoans and Mycenaeans had any

[4] Louise Schofield, *The Mycenaeans*, J. Paul Getty Museum, 2007.

significant conflicts before 1600 BCE. There is some evidence they knew of one another and traded though, which would mean their contact was a regular occurrence. The Mycenaean invasion of Minoan territory was likely not for any personal reason: The Mycenaean emphasis on power and conquest meant it would have been a wise decision to dominate a weaker neighbor like the Minoans.

Similarities and Differences

People tend to mix up the Minoans with the Mycenaeans because of their similarities, but there were several distinct differences between the two civilizations. In particular was each one's method of rising to power. While the Minoans built an empire based on trade and craftsmanship, the Mycenaeans fought and scrapped their way throughout the Aegean and Mediterranean. The Mycenaean economy was not mercantile; it relied on conquest to bring in valuable goods and keep their civilization functioning. Following the eruptions on Thera and a general decline, the Minoans became a prime candidate for more domination.

Chapter 3 – Society, Culture, and Daily Life

Information about the Minoans is scarce when compared to the wealth of knowledge scholars possess about other ancient Mediterranean civilizations. However, they still know quite a bit about general social structure, the economy, and what daily life might have been like for the average Minoan. Because of their small population, the Minoans tended to be more egalitarian than their larger neighbors, allowing opportunities for social advancement and even granting men and women similar rights. The average individual in Minoan society would have been relatively young due to lower ages of mortality, be married and have a family, perform some form of physical labor, and participate in the same religion as their neighbors. The specifics of their lives would look something like this.

Social Structure and Economy

Much of the information about the Minoans comes from images so the social structure can be difficult to ascertain. However, the

Minoan society shared some characteristics with other ancient civilizations. In particular, there were different socioeconomic classes which indicated a person's wealth and authority over others. Kings continued to be the highest position, and there were also the priestesses, priests, and administrators. One unique aspect of the Minoan world was that women held similar positions to men and were frequently depicted in positions of authority.[5] This makes sense since priestesses held more sway than the priests. Several pictures also show seated women above men, but no existing ones show seated men above women.

The Minoan economy also seemed to be based around commerce. Since they lived on islands throughout the Mediterranean Sea, the Minoans needed to travel across the water to interact with other cultures and trade. Discovered manufactured goods indicate that the Minoans most likely had contact and trade with the Mycenaeans, Egyptians, Mesopotamians, and others. Fish and other goods from the sea were common Minoan products, as was saffron and bronze sculptures. The Minoans traded for things they could not produce themselves or didn't have access to in their island civilization, including advanced weaponry, new textiles, and even cats from Egypt.[6] Minoan civilization, because it relied so heavily on commerce, started to decline when the rival Mediterranean power, the Mycenaeans, started to take over Minoan trade routes. Historians believe that the Minoans and Mycenaeans did have peaceful relations before the sudden attacks occurred.

The Roles of Men and Women

The Minoans were unusual among the ancient cultures. A recurring trend in human civilization was that as people became more urbanized, gender equality faded. A fact few know is that humans did not always have disparate gender roles in part because of the difficulty of survival. Before centralized agriculture and animal

---

[5] Ellen Adams, *Cultural Identity in Minoan Crete: Social Dynamics in the Neopalatial Period,* New York: Cambridge University Press, 2017.
[6] Castleden, *Minoans.*

husbandry, nomadic peoples tended to be more egalitarian in how they conducted themselves. Even monogamy was not common. With the development of agriculture, it was possible for humans to focus less on survival or constant travel and more on the building of stagnant civilizations. Stagnant here means a society that did not need to migrate and travel. These more stable societies led to the rise of powerful figures like kings, administrators, generals, warlords, priests, and others. These important officials tended to be male, which led to the gradual shifting of roles and the removal of rights and important roles from women.

These shifts can be seen in many of the ancient civilizations, including ones from Africa, the Middle East, Asia, and Europe. The Minoans were a special case, though. It's possible that the small size of the Minoan civilization meant that urbanization did not result in the stripping of roles from women. Indeed, Minoan artwork and existing artifacts indicate that the men and women actually possessed similar rights and roles, though it's obviously unclear since written text is limited. Some historians even believe that the Minoans were a matriarchal society, one where women were in charge rather than men. The predominance of female leaders and priestesses are what led to this speculation. Another possibility is since the Minoans would not have had a land army but instead a navy, the men would have frequently been away for long periods of time. This meant women would need to do double duty at home while they were gone.

Minoan women appeared to have more rights, opportunities, and freedoms than their counterparts in similar cultures like the Mycenaeans and the ancient Greeks. Childrearing and raising was not their sole job. Many free women seemed to hold regular jobs or were the high priestesses and temple attendants of the Minoan religion. They could even become craftswomen and hold important positions or participate in sports like the significant bull jumping. Elegant women can be frequently seen in Minoan frescos and art as priestesses or in agricultural roles like saffron gatherers, those who picked and cared for saffron crops. An example found in Santorini can be seen below.

Fresco of a Saffron Gatherer

Men had similar roles and freedoms. Although there were a few different socioeconomic classes and limited upward mobility, these did not preclude men from being able to improve themselves and hold a variety of positions. Men might be soldiers, craftsmen, farmers, laborers, nobles, priests, or administrators. The Minoan civilization was small, so urbanization meant everyone jumbled together and had more options and possibilities available to them. Men also participated in sports like bull jumping and might have been saffron gatherers, but it's ambiguous. Men did not have a large role in childrearing and instead focused on working outside of the home.

Saffron

Archaeologists and anthropologists alike believe saffron possessed a unique position in Minoan culture. Saffron crocus is a plant commonly known as the *crocus sativus* and is characterized by its purple color and strands of crimson styles that poke from the center. Both the Minoans and modern societies pluck the styles from the saffron to create spices and dyes. Minoan art depicts saffron as being a common wild plant, but it no longer grows outside of carefully cultivated farms and gardens. In ancient times, it was also used as a medicine. The Minoans frequently depicted saffron in association with women in a sort of production line, indicating it was harvested for common use.[7]

Several scholars speculate that the first goddess of medicine in the Mediterranean world came from the Minoans living on the island of Thera. The murals and other artwork discovered on the island include drawings of a female goddess surrounded by botanically accurate depictions of the saffron plant and its unique properties compared to other flora that grew on the island.[8] It's believed that the Minoans thought that saffron was special for treating medical conditions as well as for dyes, spices, and other uses.

Food and Diet

As can be imagined, the Minoan diet consisted of a wide variety of seafood and products taken from the Mediterranean. Their island home meant large-scale agriculture was out of the question, especially since the population focused on growing crops of saffron to treat illnesses. This meant the primary source of consumable goods was the waters of the Mediterranean itself, as well as nearby groups that the Minoans could trade with for sustenance.

---

[7] J.S., "Saffron and the Minoans.," *Pharmacy in History* 47, no. 1 (2005): pg. 28-31. https://www.jstor.org/stable/41112251.

[8] S.C. Ferrence and G. Bendersky, "Therapy with saffron and the goddess at Thera," *Perspectives in Biology and Medicine* 47, no. 2 (Spring 2004): pg. 199-226. https://www.ncbi.nlm.nih.gov/pubmed/15259204.

A known delicacy was young squid, which could be caught and served raw or cooked to remove parasites. Squid ink was also used to flavor foods or give color to dyes. Numerous varieties of fish, clams, and other fresh meat additionally came from the sea. These were combined with a broad range of agricultural crops that could be cultivated in the rocky terrain and a variety of vegetables. These vegetables were not grown like regular agricultural crops. Instead of being planted in large groups, they were confined to smaller household gardens. Some of the most popular vegetables were peas, lentils, field beans, asparagus, wild artichokes, wild mustard, okra, and endives. These vegetables tended to have bitter, sharp tastes that lent themselves well to fresh meat.

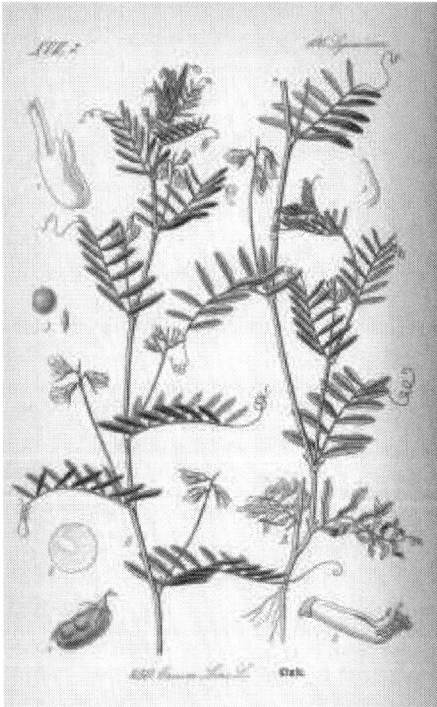

The Lentil Plant

The Mediterranean climate was also conducive to growing multiple varieties of grapes and olives, which the Minoans used to make wine and olive oil. Their wine tended to have a low alcoholic content because the fermentation process was used to eliminate bacteria and waterborne parasites rather than create a fun beverage. However, the Minoans did also produce wine with high alcohol content for special occasions, libations during religious ceremonies, and general consumption. Other popular drinks were barley beer, mead, and wines seasoned and flavored with herbs. The Minoans also made a mild milk drink flavored with local herbs as well. Drinking vessels found on Crete contain the faint remnants of ancient wine that appear to have been flavored with toasted oak wood to give it a sharper, smokier flavor.

Olive oil, meanwhile, was eaten with grains and vegetables and provided a major source of nutrition and calories for the general public. Olives could also be consumed from the tree. Aside from vegetables, the Minoans did grow some grains. They managed to cultivate barley, rye, and three separate types of wheat. These were typically not made into bread but could be eaten as a porridge or turned into beer.

Like most ancient peoples, the Minoans mastered animal domestication and appeared to own sheep, cattle, goats, and some pigs. These animals wouldn't have been eaten all the time; while most contemporary societies use domesticated animals as a primary source of meat, the Minoans would have needed the animals to provide usable resources like wool and milk. Goat milk was more popular than that of cows, and sheep were needed for the wool to make clothes. Pigs seem to be one of the only large mammals whose purpose was solely for food. The Minoans primarily used goat milk to make sharp-flavored but physically soft white cheeses similar to those made by the ancient Greeks. An example in contemporary times would be the modern feta.

Feta Cheese

In addition to domesticated animals, the Minoans consumed creatures they could hunt like rabbits and boar. There is evidence that the Minoans kept dogs and cats to help them hunt and keep their homes free of pests. The cats most likely came from Egypt and were traded in exchange for goods from the Mediterranean.

Fashion

The Minoans made unusual and complex fashion choices based heavily on the Mediterranean climate. Most garments were sewn in a similar manner to contemporary clothing, with blouses, skirts, and dresses being fitted to the body and designed to accentuate the waist on men and women. Fabric was made from lightweight materials like linen, although wool was not uncommon in rural areas. Men typically wore simple loincloths with the occasional draping robe. These loincloths were decorated and often included a pagne, or sheath, that protected the penis and drew attention to the individual's masculinity. As time went on, men's garments became more modest and often included tasseled aprons that covered the front and back of the hips and thighs. Toward the end of the Late Minoan Period, men started to wear simple tunics and robes that protected the upper body as well.[9]

When archaeologists discovered examples of women's garments on Crete, they were astonished by the similarities between the ancient clothing and modern dress. A woman's skirt tended to be fitted and cinched around the waist before flaring out in a popular bell shape that accentuated the female figure. Decorations and embroidery were often sewn onto the skirts to add character, and designs grew more elaborate as time wore on. Some designs featured long strips of fabric sewn into the sides of the skirts to create vertical ruffles along the length of the material. Their tops were not modest. Most women wore fitted garments with large vertical openings in the front that exposed the entire breast and the ideal slim waist. There is some evidence to suggest that men and women were fitted with tight metal belts from childhood to further accentuate a slender midsection.[10]

Minoan fashion was based around having the ideal Minoan figure, which meant exposing the waist, muscular arms and chests, or large breasts and hips with a defined waist. Some historians noted that the ideal feminine shape was similar to European fashions in the 1800s CE when women wore corsets and padded their skirts to achieve a rounded, full look. One ancient Minoan painting earned the nickname "La Parisienne" because of the female character's similarities to the fashions of French women.

---

[9] Bernice R. Jones, "Revealing Minoan Fashions," *Archaeology* 53, no. 3 (May/June 2000): pg. 36-41. https://www.jstor.org/stable/41779314.
[10] Ibid.

The Parisienne

This fresco highlights some other characteristics of Minoan fashion that were present in larger urban centers like Knossos. Archaeologists discovered what appeared to be beautification centers in palace complexes and objects that seemed to be used to accentuate features deemed attractive by the Minoans. Nobles would use natural mixtures and compounds to lighten their skin and paint their lips red, providing a contrast to the tanned skin of laborers and other lower-class individuals. Women would also wear elaborate knots and tie their hair back in creative designs, and both men and women wore jewelry made from gold, silver, or bronze to indicate their wealth and social status. Semi-precious stones, minerals, and other objects could be inlaid in the metal; popular choices were garnet, lapis lazuli, soapstone, ivory, and shells taken from the Mediterranean. The Minoans frequently traded with the Egyptians to obtain a material called Egyptian blue as well.

Were the Minoans Peaceful?

A running theory about the Minoans is that they were a peaceful civilization. This theory was first put forth by Arthur Evans, the archaeologist who discovered some of the greatest deposits of artifacts of the Minoans. According to Evans, the *Pax Minoica* (Minoan Peace) existed. This peace explained that there was little to no conflict in Minoan civilization until they came face to face with the Mycenaeans on mainland Greece. More contemporary scholars dispute Evans' idea as idealism, but the fact remains that there is no surviving evidence of a legitimate Minoan army, any form of domination beyond the island of Crete, or even warfare. Artwork, which depicts numerous aspects of life like saffron cultivation, has no indication that warfare existed. Violence seemed dedicated to sports and potentially ritual sacrifices.

The idea of Minoan peace is partially based on architectural evidence discovered on islands like Crete. Although archaeologists found some fortifications and watchtowers, such buildings do not indicate actual warfare. This is because most ancient fortified sites served more than one function. They could be used as storage areas, indicate important borders such as those of the palaces, or express the wealth of powerful officials. Some fortresses also served as significant gathering places or areas where people could go during harsh weather, natural disasters, and other problems. However, scholars cannot rule out warfare, especially since the Minoans did make numerous weapons that could not be used for hunting. More confusing was the presence of intimidating longboats and rapiers, which were standard weapons used for war by ancient civilizations.[11]

---

[11] Barry P.C. Molloy, "Martial Minoans? War as Social Process, Practice and Event in Bronze Age Crete," *The Annual of the British School at Athens* 107 (2012): pg. 87-142. https://www.jstor.org/stable/41721880.

Chapter 4 – Trade and Shipbuilding on the Mediterranean Sea

The Minoan civilization is called a thalassocracy, or a political state that relies on its navy to guarantee population safety and unite different regions of the same culture. Scholars can tell that the Minoans shored up their navy and built dozens of trading vessels designed to facilitate commerce with places all across the Mediterranean.[12] Crete was the center of their commercial industry, including the palace settlement of Knossos on the east coast of the island. Craftspeople tended to sell their finished goods like pottery and ceramics overseas. The Minoans did not produce enough agricultural products or foodstuffs to develop any major consumable

---

[12] Malcom H. Weiner, "Realities of Power: The Minoan Thalassocracy in Historical Perspective," *AMILLA: The Quest for Excellence*, 2013, http://www.academia.edu/30141237/_Realities_of_Power_The_Minoan_Thalassoc racy_in_Historical_Perspective_AMILLA_The_Quest_for_Excellence._Studies_Pre sented_to_Guenter_Kopcke_in_Celebration_of_His_75th_Birthday_2013_pp._149 _173

trade, and records show that the citizens might have even traded their finished products for surplus crops in places like Egypt.

Year round, merchants would gather goods that could be traded to places like Egypt, Mesopotamia, mainland Greece, Anatolia, and even Spain. Minoan art and other objects have been found in all five locations. As a maritime civilization, it's believed the Minoans owed the majority of their success to being able to trade for goods and luxuries that would have been unavailable on Santorini and Crete.

Map of the Mediterranean Sea

The Minoans had little need for an army because of their location. The majority of people lived in relatively undefended coastal cities protected by large fleets of seafaring vessels. Minoan ships featured modifications and weapons to protect traders and settlements from pirates, but archaeologists note that these additions to the ships are almost always unused and untouched. This fact helps support Arthur Evans' idea about the "Minoan Peace," or the theory that the Minoans as a culture did not need to engage in warfare with their neighbors and experienced little fighting or aggression.

Two of the goods the Minoans were known for were tin and saffron. Tin was a necessary material for the making of bronze weapons and armor during the Bronze Age. Minoan miners gathered the metal from Cyprus, where it could be alloyed with copper to make rough bronze for shipping to other civilizations. Saffron, meanwhile, grew rampant in places like Akrotiri on Santorini. The plant was highly sought after in the ancient world for its taste, color, and supposed medicinal properties. Some records indicate that the Minoans might have even completed the process of using saffron as a dye for fabrics before shipment, although there is not enough evidence to support the presence of large-scale textile production. Luxury resources like gold and silver taken from small Mediterranean islands also formed valuable goods that the Minoans could trade.

Minoan Fleet

All commerce in the thalassocracy needed to be protected by the Minoan fleet. Unlike the ships of other seafaring civilizations, the Minoan fleet was not designed to engage in heavy warfare or conquest. Each vessel's primary purpose appeared to be trade with extra weapons added to defend goods from pirates. Before the Mycenaeans, the Minoans did not fight their neighbors and thus had little use for a dedicated navy.

Minoan Fleet Fresco

Frescos, like the one above, provide an excellent example of what the standard Minoan ship looked like. Shipbuilders created longboats using wood and bronze tools. These longboats were roughly thirty-five meters (114.8 ft.) long and six meters wide (19.7 ft.). Each ship was capable of carrying 50 metric tons worth of goods and could be manned by fifty people rowing the oars that stuck out on either side of the vessel. There was extra room for individuals like the captain and his specialty crew who were capable of repairing the ship in case of emergency.

The Minoans possessed a clear process for the creation of a ship capable of traversing the Mediterranean. Trees were a finite resource on their islands, so the Minoans saved larger ones for the building of boats. Entire cypress trunks were favored because the shipbuilders could shave off excess bark and material using massive bronze saws that measured roughly 6 ft. in length and 1 ft. wide. The process consisted of a few deceptively simple but physically challenging steps.

1. Professionals would identify a tree with good characteristics and chop it down using bronze axes.

2. The branches would then be removed, and the tree would be transported by rudimentary wagons to a shipbuilding center on one of the coasts.

3. The cypress bark would be stripped from the tree using basic wooden or bronze scrapers.

4. Clean logs would then be marked by the master shipbuilder so he and his workers (shipbuilding was primarily a male profession due to the strength required) could identify where cuts needed to be made.

5. Once the marks were made, the shipbuilding team started to cut, slice, and saw away extra wood. The finished product would be one solid boat with few to no attached pieces. This created sturdy construction and prevented leaks.

6. The upward curves on the bow and stern (the front and rear of the boat, respectively) were pushed into shape by making the wood malleable by heat and steam.

7. Extra bands of cypress were then added to the completed shell of the ship using the process of edge-joining. Mortises, or rectangular notches, were cut into the boat, and then notches and the slabs of wood were joined together. Resins were used to prevent slippage and seal any major cracks or gaps that could let water into the boat. The mortises would become fully sealed when the ship was pushed into the seawater upon completion.

8. The process of adding extra cypress bands was used all around the ship to give the vessel needed height and protection from the waters of the Mediterranean. Once the banding was completed, the shipbuilder would add rowing benches and decking for the sailors.

9. Completed ships were then covered in white woven linen and decorated with pictures of blue dolphins and other creatures of the sea.

The Striped Dolphin – The Minoans' Favorite Animal

Those nine steps created the basic ship the Minoans would have used for trading. Oars for rowing were made from oak, which was more solid and heavier than the cypress used for the boat's frame. Some shipbuilders would add masts and sails to the completed vessels, so the seafarers did not need to rely solely on manpower to travel across the Mediterranean. Masts were made with oak and tended to be a whopping 52.5 ft. tall. Sails were made of wool and treated with oil to be waterproof.[13]

Such simple vessels were not meant to carry complicated weapons. Frescos indicate that the defensive measures against pirates were probably fundamental additions like long spears that would be held by sailors along the sides of the ship. This would have stopped pirates or other invaders from boarding and taking trade goods. Most crewmembers also carried basic weapons like knives that could double as tools and eating utensils.

Ultimately, the Minoans' role as a maritime civilization can be seen in the simplicity and beauty of their ships. The vessels did not include massive defensive constructs or weapons and featured a basic open-air design that favored the sunny climate of the Mediterranean. Manpower was needed to move the ships across the sea, and the sailors provided the only line of defense against enemies. However, they did not appear to engage in combat often. This idea is supported not only by the simple design but also the immense amount of time spent painting and decorating completed vessels. Ships were works of art to the Minoans, often sporting their favorite dolphin and bird motifs. These designs made the vessels attractive, alerted potential commercial partners to the wealth of the Minoans, and made the ships conspicuous on the waters. As some scholars say, if the Minoans were worried about attack, would they have made their trading vessels so distinct and undefended?

---

[13] Cemal Pulak and George F. Bass, "Bronze Age Shipwreck Excavation at Uluburun," Institute of Nautical Archaeology.

Chapter 5 – Language and Linear A

Multiple writing systems dating from the time of the Minoans have been found in Crete and Santorini, although most of them are undeciphered. The first known written script for the Minoans was something called the Cretan hieroglyphs. Scholars are unsure if these hieroglyphs were actually used by the Minoans, and their entire origin is debated. However, they were used before Linear A and can be found in the regions where the Minoans lived, having appeared sometime during the 19th century BCE. The Cretan hieroglyphs were also used at the same time as Linear A and disappeared around the 17th century BCE when they appeared to fall out of favor.

A Jaspar Seal with Cretan Hieroglyphics (c. 1800s BCE)

After the Cretan hieroglyphs came the two most well-known writing systems, Linear A and Linear B. Linear A came before Linear B and is considered its parent, or the writing system on which Linear B was based. Linear B was not used by the Minoans. Linear A dates from 2500 BCE and 1450 BCE and is almost unintelligible to contemporary scholars due to the incompleteness of preserved documents and the language used in the script. However, Linear A is frequently called Minoan, and multiple professionals believe the language is the written form of the Minoan spoken word. Although there are some similarities to ancient Greek, there are not enough.

An Example of Linear A

Scholars attempted to translate the values of Linear B into Linear A to create an example of the language, but the result was unintelligible. This translation process took the values of the symbols in Linear B and then applied them to their known counterpart in Linear A. This procedure would be similar to someone taking the sound associated with the letter "R" and applying it to the Cyrillic equivalent, which is "P." However, the result did not make sense, indicating that the Minoan language might not have been related to any known languages. There is a current belief that the Minoans actually did not use their written alphabet to record their language and instead used it for accounting.

Another form of writing discovered in the region of the Minoans is a script found on an artifact called the Phaistos Disc. The Phaistos Disc was found at the ruins of the palace complex of Phaistos on the southern coast of Crete. Luigi Pernier, an Italian archaeologist, found the disc in the basement. It measures 5.9 in. in diameter and was found in an area full of items like bovine bones. Scholars believe that the rooms were used for general storage and appeared to collapse upon themselves following the Therian eruption.

The Phaistos Disc contains images of a pictorial script that hasn't been found in any other location. Archaeologists now believe it to be of Cretan origin and is currently indecipherable. Examples of the symbols can be seen transcribed in the image below.

The Writing on the Phaistos Disc

In short, modern scholars can't tell what the Minoan language actually sounded like, but there is some evidence for what it looked like. Similar to other ancient civilizations, the Minoans did not have much use for a written script. Almost everyone was illiterate and would have no need to read or write. The only people who did would have been court scribes, traders, and some members of the religious class. This is why the majority of documents carrying Linear A script are accounting records.

Chapter 6 – The Potential Predecessors of Greek Religion

Archaeologists, historians, and other scholars believe that the Minoans developed the elements that would evolve into the future ancient Greek religion. Some of the religious objects discovered at sites like Crete include paintings, statuettes, and seal rings that point to a specific cultic practice revolving around influential gods, goddesses, and a class of priests and priestesses. As mentioned earlier, the Minoans were unique among ancient cultures in that their religion emphasized and elevated women in its practice. Surviving artifacts and imagery indicate that priestesses held the most essential roles in worship and had more power than their male counterparts. Evidence further points toward the chief Minoan deity being a woman rather than a man. This is the famous snake goddess.

The Snake Goddess

Based on evidence, archaeologists and anthropologists believe the most significant deity in the Minoan religion was a goddess associated with snakes. Sometimes artists would also depict her with bulls, lions, or doves, significant animals in religions throughout the ancient world. This figure appeared to have some form of medical significance as women would leave offerings of saffron, their all-purpose plant, at her altars. In images, the goddess can sometimes be seen with a smaller, younger man whom archaeologists believe was either her consort or son. Although there were no formal public temples, the goddess would be worshiped and attended to by priestesses.

Archaeologists suspect that the deity would be co-opted in ancient Greek religion and depicted as Ariadne, the daughter of the famous King Minos from whom the Minoans take their name. In tablets taken from Knossos, the goddess is sometimes referred to as the "mistress of the labyrinth." These documents are written in Linear B, the language of the Mycenaean Greeks, rather than Linear A. This could indicate that civilizations like the Mycenaeans and the ancient Greeks adapted the preexisting Minoan religion into their own pantheons.[14]

The Two Snake Goddess Figurines Found in 1903

The original snake goddess figurine was discovered by Arthur Evans in 1903 and depicted an obviously female individual with a snake in either hand. Snakes did not have a negative connotation for the

---

[14] Castledon, *Minoans.*

Minoans and seemed to indicate domesticity, the household, motherhood, and potentially healing and mastery over nature and animals. Evans originally postulated that the larger of the discovered figurines was a goddess while the smaller was a priestess. These particular statuettes have only been found in household shrines and other domesticate places, which is why archaeologists suspect the goddess was associated with the home. However, mentions to an overarching, powerful snake goddess could also be found in shrines throughout the Minoan landscape, leaving the situation vague.

The Sacral Knot

The sacral knot was a discovery by Evans at Knossos. This knot had a loop on top and two fringed ends that hung below. It appeared multiple times in Minoan figurines, mainly on the two snake goddess statuettes. The knot sat between their breasts and could be seen throughout Minoan religious artifacts in a variety of materials. Evans speculated that the sacral knot was an important religious symbol similar to the double-edged axe, which also occurred everywhere where the Minoans settled.

The Double-Bitted or Double-Edged Axe

The double-bitted axe was a common symbol that appeared in almost every religious site discovered in Minoan territory. Its appearance is self-explanatory: the axe had a blade on either side of the handle and was ceremonial. The axe can be found in the religious symbolism of numerous cultures across the Mediterranean in the ancient world. Contrary to its representation in other cultures though, the double-bitted axe in Minoan religion only ever appeared with female figures and did not represent a weapon or military conquest. Some scholars believe the axe was representative of the origin of the known world because of its shape, and others associate it with the significant female goddess mentioned earlier.

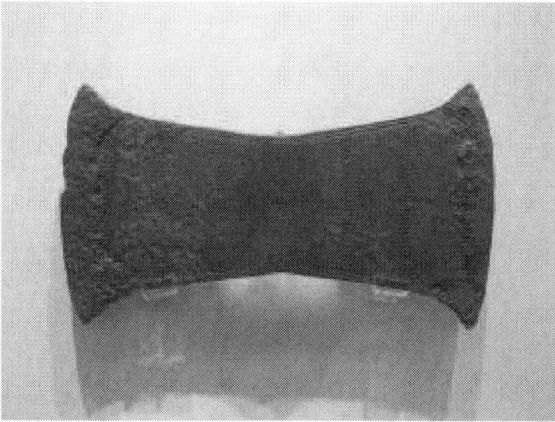

The Arkalochori Axe (c. 2000 BCE)

The double-bitted axe did not only appear as a symbol. Some artifacts have been found, including the Arkalochori Axe dating back to the second millennium BCE. The bronze votive axe was excavated by the Greek archaeologist Spyridon Marinatos in 1934. Inscribed along the edges are fifteen symbols that some suspect is Linear A, but the material is too degraded to clearly make out the forms. Archaeologists think the axe was used during religious ceremonies and, again, was not a weapon. The axe can currently be found at the Heraklion Archaeological Museum.

The Practice of Worship: A Cultic Structure

Religious artifacts are some of the most enduring objects for the Minoans. Some of the numerous items found include metal and clay votive figures, figurines of animals and humans, special double axes, and miniatures of objects that the Minoans would have used in their daily lives. Archaeologists and anthropologists have also found over 300 separate shrines and caves filled with sacred items that might have been the centers of a prominent religious cult. This version of a cult does not have the same negative connotations of modern-day cults. When used in the discussion of ancient history, the word "cult" simply refers to a small group that worshiped a particular deity or figure, or a form of religious worship that was not officially organized or mainstream.

Temples, as contemporary audiences know them, were not a concept among the Minoans, and there were no clear sites of buildings used for formal, organized worship. It's speculated that the Minoans instead selected and educated priestesses, and sometimes priests, who then conducted ceremonies and rituals for supportive groups at open-air sites. These sites would have been the temples of the Minoans. Palace complexes did not have designated religious spaces, and no surviving Minoan frescos show any deities. The only indicators tend to be the consistent statuettes, which depict the same woman bearing two snakes, one in each hand.

Interestingly, there was one unique cultic figure that baffled archaeologists when first discovered. This was something called the Minoan Genius. It is best described as a strange creature that blends the characteristics of a lion and a hippo. Scholars have noted that there are numerous similarities between the Minoan Genius and some of the fantastic animals depicted in ancient Egyptian art, and they think the animal demonstrates a connection between the two cultures. In the Minoan religion, the Genius seemed to be a protector of children as well as an important figure during fertility rituals. They were also frequently shown with ewers, or water pitchers, and seemed to play a significant role in the giving of libations during religious ceremonies.

Two Minoan Genii

Bull-Leaping

Bull-leaping clearly held some significance among the Minoans as it was a popular subject for frescos, pottery, and even scenes inscribed upon pieces of jewelry. In bull-leaping, an enterprising athlete had to leap over a charging bull by seizing the horns, propelling themselves up, and landing on the animal's back. Artwork indicates that men and women both participated in such events and that winners were lauded.

Knossos – Bull-Leaping Fresco

Whether the activity possessed any sort of ritualistic, religious, or cultic belief is debated. Bull-leaping was clearly a popular subject and seemed to possess some rituals of its own, but the images don't tend to be found in temples. Some scholars of the ancient world draw connections between the depicted bulls and the Sacred Bull, a popular feature in ancient religions. This Sacred Bull was considered a symbol of awe and power and tended to be associated with the chief or supreme deity of the religion. For the Minoans, an argument can be made for a connection between the bull and the snake goddess mentioned earlier.

Others go on to argue that the bulls had no significance and that the artwork isn't even depicting bull-leaping. They claim that the scenes are actually somewhat humorous: they are stills of young men and women attempting to ride a bull for the first time and failing miserably.[15]

The Existence of Human Sacrifice

Did the Minoans participate in human sacrifice?

Maybe.

There are three chief sites where archaeologists believe they have found evidence to support the idea of ritualistic human sacrifice: Anemospilia, a complex at Fournou Korifi, and a building in Knossos known as the North House. Findings at each location are inclusive and might not actually be from sacrifice, but the sites are suspicious enough to give scholars pause. In order of the plausibility of found evidence, the least likely to be an incident of human sacrifice is the scene found at Anemospilia.

Anemospilia

Anemospilia presents an interesting situation for archaeologists. The site is a temple destroyed by the earthquake during the Middle

---

[15] Nanno Marinatos, "Minoan Religion," Columbia: University of South Carolina, 1993.

Minoan period. Inside were the remains of a cult statue as well as four human skeletons: two men, one woman, and one unidentifiable. One of the male skeletons was trussed into a contorted, contracted position on a raised platform that would have been painful to force oneself into. A bronze blade was discovered inside his pile of bones. The fifteen-inch knife featured depictions of bulls, a sacred animal, on either side. Discoloration on one side of the bones indicated the man most likely died of blood loss before the earthquake hit. Two skeletons were found in varying stages of surprise around the strange victim. Archaeologists believe they were startled when the earthquake hit, and their crushed bones mean the temple collapsed during the ritual.

The skeleton of indeterminate gender was discovered in one of the halls of the temple with over a hundred pottery fragments around them. Discoloration again indicated the jar they were carrying was full of blood. The archaeologists who excavated the scene never gave an official report on their findings, and the only major published document is an old article from *National Geographic* published in 1981.

Although professionals speculate, many believe Anemospilia was not a scene of human sacrifice. Some claim the man who bled out might have been dying from a wound received at sea and that the blade had been placed upon his body as a symbol of honor. Others go along with this idea and think the entire situation was a funerary rite gone wrong. Finally, quite a few people think the entire scene was caused by the earthquake and that it's likely the supposed sacrifice victim bled out from injuries caused by falling debris. The knife resembles a spearhead, which could have easily fallen from a shelf and pierced the seventeen-year-old's ribcage.

The next site is a sanctuary complex at Fournou Korifi. Here, fragments from a human skull were recovered from a chamber containing a variety of cooking equipment and a hearth. The archaeologists believe the skull was the remains of some form of human sacrifice, but the situation is—to put it simply—iffy. When working with ancient remains, the strangest things can turn up. In this situation, it's likely that the skull came from an individual who died in their kitchen or cooking area. The only caveat to this theory is that the rest of the skeleton was not found in the area. This gives rise to the idea that the human head was transported to the cooking area for potentially nefarious reasons.

Finally, there's Knossos. If there was going to be evidence of Minoan human sacrifice, ignoring the logistics of trying to find material culture from a civilization from millennia ago, it would be in Knossos. The administrative, cultural, and religious capital of the Minoans, Knossos included numerous mass burial sites where archaeologists discovered almost definitive evidence of child sacrifice. Findings indicate the victims were most likely cannibalized by their killers.[16]

The evidence of ritualistic human sacrifice comes from the stripping of the flesh from bones in a manner similar to sacrificed animals. All of the children in the burial site appeared to be healthy, so the chances of them being sick or left to die are unlikely. The archaeologists who excavated the site along with other professionals think the sacrifice might have been part of a cultic ritual wherein children were slaughtered, cooked, and then eaten as a way to renew and improve fertility in the coming year. Sometimes to have a child, one must apparently kill one.[17]

No one knows how subjects for sacrifice were chosen. Dating the skeletons reveals that almost all of the victims were below eighteen years of age with preference given to young, healthy individuals. Flesh and blood were taken from the victims, and as mentioned before, there is some evidence of cannibalization. That the Minoans might have engaged in such behavior is not surprising since many ritualistic cults from the Stone, Bronze, and even early Iron Ages

---

[16] Castledon, *Minoans*.

[17] Peter Warren, "Knossos: New Excavations and Discoveries," *Archaeology* (July /August 1984): p. 48-55.

included such practices. Without a doubt, humans all around the world have sacrificed and eaten one another to appease nature or the gods.

But what does this say about Minoan religion?

On the one hand, evidence of sacrifice demonstrates the power of cultic beliefs as well as a presence of preordained rituals that needed to be complete. Historians do not know why, but they can tell that what religious practices the Minoans did have were important to them and required special sites, priestesses, priests, and specialized implements like the bronze bull knife.

Burial and Mortuary Practices

Burial remains constitute many of the artifacts from the Bronze Age because ancient peoples tended to follow strict, ritualistic behaviors during funerals and did their best to preserve the bodies of their beloved. For the Minoans, many of the remains come from the time of the Middle Minoans and from the island of Crete. Remains were kept in either house tombs or burial tombs and followed the technique of inhumation. A site at Ayia Photia bears evidence of being a chamber reserved specifically for dead children. The Minoans did not appear to cremate their deceased but did bury more than one person in a single gravesite. Archaeologists speculate that bodies buried in the same plot were either related or members of a public tomb. Wealthy or notable families possessed crypts while poorer individuals made do with public cemeteries or their own land.

In general, families attempted to leave their deceased grave goods and furniture. No one knows whether the Minoans believed the dead could take the objects into the afterlife or whether there was a ritual for placing the objects. A current theory, based on the inordinate number of cups and rhytons—cups shaped like animals—found in tombs, is that some sort of toasting ritual was a part of preparing the deceased for the burial. Other common grave goods were tools and weapons, jewelry, pottery, and special storage jars. The objects might have been related to an individual's profession or personal preferences—for example, a farmer might be buried with his or her hoe, while a wealthy noble might be laid to rest with their favorite pendant.

Trends shifted during the time of the Late Minoans. Instead of group burial plots, the Minoans favored single burials where the body was placed in a clay storage vessel or laid to rest in a clay or wooden sarcophagus. These were not stored in a built tomb. The vessel or sarcophagus would be painted and covered with scenes similar to those on frescoes, and the body itself was folded to fit into the small container. Despite the popularity of this new method, many of the deceased continued to be buried in rock-cut tombs or old family burial places.

Lasting Influence on the Mycenaeans and the Greeks

Scholars remain divided on just how much influence the Minoans might have had on the Mycenaeans and Greeks when it comes to religion. Few concrete facts about Minoan religious culture remain, and the failure of modern professionals to translate or understand Linear A means many are in the dark about deity names, domains, and even meanings. However, there is evidence that the Mycenaeans and the Greeks were familiar with Minoan tales and legends, as they utilized some common elements and incorporated Cretan names and ideas into their own mythos. The Minoans also demonstrated influence by providing the framework for several important Greek myths, including that of the Minotaur. Despite trepidation in the field, some scholars still come forward and state that the Greek goddess Athena was derived from the Minoan snake deity seen earlier. Whatever the case may be, Minoan religion remains a mystery and will continue to be so without any breakthroughs in Linear A interpretation and translation or new site excavations.

Chapter 7 – Art

Although the Minoans left few written records, their artwork stood the test of time and continues to be excavated from sites on Crete, Santorini, and the surrounding islands. Artwork, pottery, and other examples of material culture are beneficial to scholars because they demonstrate what the Minoans found important, their standards of beauty, how people were thought to look, and can even reveal societal norms and distinctions. These crafts additionally provide an insight into how technologically advanced the Minoans were, as certain techniques required skill and an understanding of the fundamental properties of metal and chemicals or compounds found in the materials. Finally, their artwork also indicates how much the Minoans traded with other civilizations and how they influenced future Aegean cultures, as the Mycenaeans and ancient Greeks copied many of the Minoan styles even centuries later.[18]

When discussing Minoan art, it's important to note that scholars only count pieces that can be dated between 2600 BCE and 1100 BCE. Anything before or after has the possibility of belonging to a

---

[18] Reynold Higgins, *Minoan and Mycenaean Art*, London: Thames and Hudson, 1997.

separate civilization. The largest collection is currently at the Heraklion Archaeological Museum near Knossos on Crete. Pieces are categorized as belonging to the Early, Middle, or Late Minoans due to some technical differences that appear.[19] Unfortunately, textiles and other degradable materials like wood have already decomposed, so the best examples of Minoan art come from the more durable products that the wealthy would have possessed as well as pottery. Pottery is ubiquitous, as almost every individual in every civilization around the world needed a jug at some point—even now. For these reasons, the best examples of Minoan art are frescos, pottery, metalwork, and jewelry.

Frescoes

A fresco is an image painted on a wall or ceiling as decoration. It can be done through numerous techniques and with a variety of materials, but frescoes are one of the oldest and most enduring art forms of human civilization. The Minoans left behind numerous examples, although one issue with their preservation is that they are inherently fragile, as sections can erode, the paint will fade away, and many of the discovered frescoes appear to have been moved from their original locations by enterprising individuals. Despite this, the frescoes demonstrate some important aspects of Minoan life, culture, and values through their choice of subjects and artistic tendencies.

---

[19] Ibid.

The Fisherman Fresco

Archaeologists and specialists in art believe the work done by the Minoans is an example of buon fresco. In this technique, the artist uses color pigments to paint on wet lime plaster. There is no binding agent, which means the plaster absorbs the paint and protects the image from fading. Professionals can detect this technique by looking at string impressions left behind in the plaster as well as the depth of the paint layers. The thickness demonstrates how the Minoans would have applied the wet paint directly without relying on extra materials.[20]

In general, Minoan frescoes possessed a three-dimensional effect and used numerous bright colors. The most popular were blue, white, red, and black, although yellow and green sometimes appeared. Shading did not seem to exist. Based on existing frescoes, professionals think the Minoans copied some of the artwork of the Egyptians by making female skin white, male skin red, and assigning different primary colors to precious metals. For example, silver was depicted as blue while bronze was red.

---

[20] M. A. S. Cameron, R. E. Jones and S. E. Philippakis, "Scientific Analyses of Minoan Fresco Samples from Knossos," *The Annual of the British School at Athens* 72 (1977): pgs. 121-184.

The Minoans depicted numerous scenes in their frescoes, many of which possessed cultural significance. Some of the most common were images of the bull leapers as well as festivals, rituals, and potentially religious ceremonies. Priestesses often appeared, as did dancers. Natural subjects and animals dotted frescoes throughout Minoan settlements with identifiable flowers like lilies and crocuses. Animals were shown in their natural habitats and included the mundane, like goats, and the mythological, like the griffin. Reeds and depictions of sea creatures like the flying fish could be found, especially in palaces. Dolphins seem to be a favorite in Minoan culture.

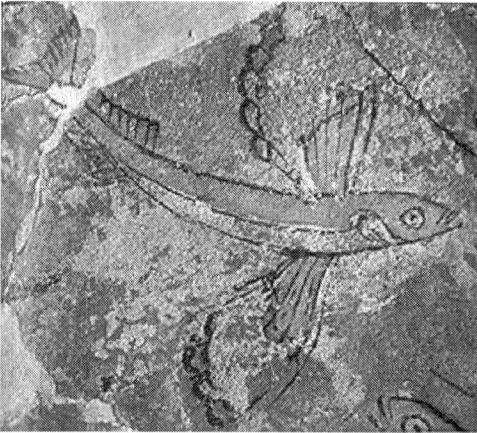

The Flying Fish Fresco

Minoan fresco techniques and subject matter lasted long after the end of their civilization. In particular, the Mycenaeans copied the Minoan fresco technique and included many of their subjects, although their artists also emphasized the importance of military and material culture. Some archaeologists also connect later Egyptian frescos with the Minoans because they contain many of the same techniques, in particular, the work in Tell el Dab'a.[21]

---

[21] Sara Cole, "The Wall Paintings of Tell el-Dab'a: Potential Aegean Connections," Pursuit - The Journal of Undergraduate Research at the University of Tennessee 1, no. 10 (2010).

Frescoes are some of the most significant artifacts for scholars because they demonstrate what was important to the Minoans. Professionals long thought the Minoans were peaceful, and part of their evidence was the clear lack of weaponry or militaristic scenes in surviving frescoes. It seemed the Minoans were content in depicting their everyday lives, beautiful men and women, and the glory of the nature around them. The incorporation of geometric patterns as well as artistic techniques from Egypt showed how much the Minoans traded and how these interactions affected their own culture. While frescoes reveal much, they share their position as the most significant surviving form of art with pottery, a ubiquitous skill that produced both mundane and elaborate pieces.

Pottery

Contemporary scholars know a ridiculous amount about Minoan pottery because so much of it has been found at sites throughout the Aegean Sea. Pottery is an important tool for dating the Minoan civilization because professionals can tell the age of the materials by examining the techniques used and the wear and tear on the surface. Artistic styles and choices of design reveal information about the different time periods in which the pottery was made, and the presence of samples throughout the Mediterranean in locations like Egypt, Syria, and Cyprus demonstrates how far the Minoans traded.[22]

The pottery discovered in and around Crete include pots, rhytons, ceramic figures, and some small statues. Pottery sarcophaguses became popular during the late Middle and Late Minoan periods and can be found full of cremated ashes, although cremation was not common. The majority of the world's Minoan pottery collection is currently at the Heraklion Archaeological Museum on Crete. Archaeologists remain unsure how pottery was produced, but it's suspected that pieces were done individually or in small quantities at

---

[22] Philip B. Betancourt, *The History of Minoan Pottery*, Princeton: Princeton University Press, 1985.

specific workshops where there was sufficient clay. Both men and women were potters and worked year-round to produce sought-after goods. Some workshops catered specifically to the palaces, while others produced objects for the general public.

Late Minoan Bull's Head Rhyton

Early Minoan pottery continued traditions from the Final Neolithic period. Objects that date back to this period tend to feature local variations that indicate there was no set pattern or technique among the Minoans at this stage. This pottery can be divided into several different types: Pyrgos Ware, Incised Ware, Agios Onouphrios, Vasiliki Ware, Fine Gray Ware, Lebena Ware, and Koumasa Ware. These classifications refer to the general form the pottery took as well as its finish, color, and potential crafting technique.

Pyrgos Ware, also known as Burnished Ware, tended to be chalices created by making a cup and attaching it to a funnel-shaped stand. Archaeologists suspect this type was used for rituals at the Pyrgos site where the chalices were excavated. The site appeared to be a rock shelter with religious significance. Pyrgos Ware would be black, brown, or gray and have a linear pattern inscribed around the piece. Incised Ware, called Scores Ware, were burnished jugs and lumpy, bulbous jars covered in incised line patterns. These can be found in northern and northeastern Crete, and scholars think the pattern might have been imported from another civilization.

Agios Onouphrios is a collection of pottery with painted parallel lines around the pieces. This type of pottery was colored with a red clay slip that could be oxidized in a kiln. This style was found in northern and southern Crete. Lebena Ware was found in the same places and was a similar style of pottery with white patterns painted on red clay. Both styles date to 2600 BCE–1900 BCE.[23]

Vasiliki Ware features a mottled glaze, some efforts at controlling color, and elongated spouts. Potters would make the mottling effect by manipulating the heat through uneven firing to create dark colors. They might have placed hot coals against the clay as well to change certain spots. Vasiliki Ware can be found in eastern Crete.

Early Minoan Vasiliki Vase, c. 2400 BCE – 2200 BCE

Finally, the Early Minoans produced Koumasa and Fine Gray Wares. Koumasa Ware is similar to Aghios Onouphrios and tends to feature red and black designs on a light clay vessel. These tend to be

---

[23] Ibid.

cups, bowls, jugs, and other drinking containers. Fine Gray Ware is similar but tends to be cylindrical with a polished surface. Potters would incise shapes onto these pots to create designs.

The Middle Minoan period saw the rise of an urbanized palace culture that required versatile vessels that could be used for storage and daily use. Pottery creation became standardized in workshops, and more elite wares were produced, creating a difference between the vessels used by nobles and those used by commoners. The pottery wheel made it to the Minoans from the Levant, and craftsmen and women became more adept at used iron-red slips of clay to add colors to vessels in insulated kilns. Out of this period came the Pithoi, which were massive storage vessels capable of holding 1,100 lbs. of liquid. Over 400 were found in the ruins of the palace of Knossos. Around this time, artisans painted fewer natural scenes and instead favored motives of geometric shapes, spirals, and elaborate whorls.

With new techniques and cultural changes came new styles of pottery. These were the Incised, the Barbotine, the Eggshell, and the Kamares. The Incised resembled the incised designs of the Early Minoans with some slight changes in subject matter. Barbotine was bulbous, with raised bumps, knobs, cones, ridges, and waves applied by adding more clay to a product to give it texture and definition. In some pieces, these designs mimicked the barnacle growth seen on boats. Eggshell Ware gets its name because the pottery is composed of paper-thin clay.

A large collection of Kamares Ware was discovered in the cave sanctuary of Kamares on Mount Ida in 1890. In the collection were some of the first polychrome vessels and evidence of pottery made on the new wheel imported from the east. These vessels tended to have light backgrounds and were covered in reds, browns, and sometimes whites to create coils, floral designs, and other shapes. Symmetry was key, but the artists tended to be creative.

A Collection of Middle Minoan Cups from Phaistos

Toward the end of the Middle Minoan period, artists turned away from their geometric designs and instead focused once more on animal and nature motifs. These could include vegetation, flowers, lilies, palms, and other local flora. Surprisingly, despite the rise of the nature designs, green was not used on pottery, perhaps because of its difficulty to mix with the materials available.

Finally, there was the pottery of the Late Minoans. Around this time, the Minoans started to influence the styles of other peoples in the Aegean Sea and exported their work as far as Egypt. The floral style from the late Middle Minoan continued, with painted red and black leaves and flowers on white backgrounds being the most popular scene. Archaeologists can tell which pieces came from which workshop because the pottery exhibits hallmarks of particular artists. Names, however, remain unknown.

Later, potters started using the Marine Style. Here, entire scenes were made of sea creatures with backgrounds of seaweed, sponges, and rocks. Octopi were some of the most iconic, and the entire style avoided structure to make the animals look like they were floating on the pot. The Marine Style is considered the last true Minoan style because the eruption of Thera followed shortly after and destroyed many of the workshops and production centers.[24]

---

[24] Ibid.

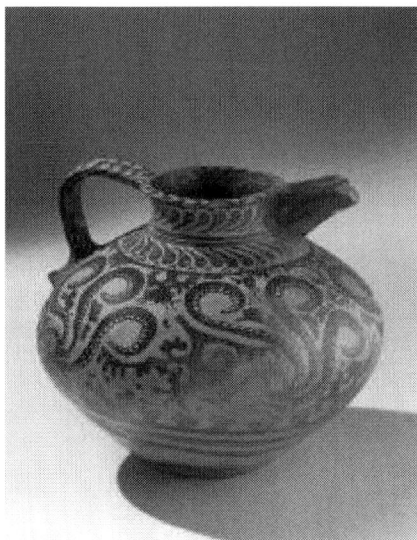

Minoan Pottery Jug, 1575 BCE–1500 BCE

This image demonstrates how important it was to Minoan artists to cover the canvas of their work with elaborate and intricate designs. This jug, produced in the 16th century BCE, features a beautiful depiction of sea life as well as simple yet opulent geometric patterns around the mouth and handle. It's likely this particular jug was meant for decoration rather than utilitarian purposes, but the artwork remains revealing nonetheless. This particular piece is an example of the Late Minoan Marine Style.

Metalwork

Still another form of artwork was metalworking, or the creation of ornaments, jewelry, and even cups from metals like gold and copper. Both materials needed to be imported, and they demonstrated the status of their owners. A common technique for metalworking was gold granulation, which allowed artists to create elaborate pieces like the famous gold bee pendant—a necklace that looks like a bee complete with wings. In order to make such items, the craftsmen and women needed to understand the basic properties of the metal and be able to manipulate fire to precise temperatures to bond gold without burning it. Such skills developed over the three Minoan periods, as the Minoans first learned to shape bronze and started to incorporate more metals as their trade networks expanded.

Archaeologists have located metal vessels on Crete that date roughly to the middle of the Early Minoan period, or c. 2500 BCE. Some of the newest metalwork comes from c. 1450, which indicates the Minoans were still producing their iconic crafts up until the fall of their civilization. The earliest examples of metalwork were made from precious metals like gold, but more recent products were made of arsenical or tin bronze. Historians suggest the adaption was the result of more individuals being able to afford metalwork as well as a greater supply of materials since precious metal objects were still being made. However, most belonged to upper-class families. Cups formed the majority of precious metal metalwork, while a more diverse array of objects could be made of bronze. These included pans, bowls, cups, lamps, basins, cauldrons, and rhytons.

The Minoans exported their metal goods to the various civilizations with whom they traded. Quite a few cups and vessels with Minoan characteristics have been found on mainland Greece. It's thought that the Minoans sold their metalwork to the Mycenaeans or gifted them elaborate pieces. Objects not traded were used at home for cooking, food storage, and perhaps toasting rituals related to the Minoan cult. Bronze and gold metalwork are frequently found in graves.

The Minoans made their metal vessels mainly through lost-wax casting or the raising of sheet metal. Stone hammers and wooden tools were used to raise hot metal into the desired shape, and extra pieces like legs and handles needed to be cast separately and then riveted onto the body of a piece. Metalsmiths knew how to inlay additional precious metals, gilded vessels, and add numerous decorations like marine life, bulls, flowers, and geometric shapes.

Jewelry

The Minoans made and wore jewelry inspired by nature, with the most popular designs including flowers, animals, and bees. Their techniques and choices were influenced by the civilizations and cultures they traded with, including the Babylonians and Egyptians. Numerous deposits of these luxury goods were discovered by archaeologists on multiple islands because of the durability of the metal. One of the largest collections of jewelry was a part of the Aegina Treasure, a hoard of precious gold found on the island of Aegina. All of the jewelry included gold, either as the primary material or as an accent to beads. The collection featured four rings for fingers, three diadems, a chest pendant or brooch, two pairs of earrings, at least five additional and non-wearable rings, a golden cup, a solid gold bracelet, and numerous decorative strips.[25]

Since their islands included deposits of natural metals and resources like silver and bronze, the Minoans were able to mine materials and then refine the practices of smelting and metalwork.[26] Because of the delicate nature of jewelry making, most craftsmen and craftswomen completed individual pieces by hand. The main exceptions were when someone wanted to create rings or individual beads for necklaces. Due to the minuscule nature of these pieces, the Minoans relied on a technique called lost-wax casting.

The process of lost-wax casting dates before the Minoans to the Late Cycladic era. The golden ibex above was found in Santorini and, while perhaps not Minoan, used the same process to be created as the Minoans would use to make metal structures like beads. In lost-wax casting, a wax mold would be created with a hollowed design in the interior. The mold would be sealed, and molten material would be poured through an opening near the top. The metal would harden and take shape in the mold, resulting in elaborate objects and designs that could be remade over and over.[27]

---

[25] R. Higgins, *The Aegina Treasure - An Archaeological Mystery*, London: 1979.

[26] Although the Minoans were able to extract some gold from the ground, the majority of their supply came from trade with North Africa, where the metal was more common.

[27] J.V. Noble, "The Wax of the Lost Wax Process". *American Journal of Archaeology*, 79, no. 4 (1975).

Gold Ibex Statue c. 17ᵗʰ Century BCE (Santorini)

So, what did the Minoans like to use in their jewelry?

Precious metals tended to form the base of all pieces. Wealthier individuals could afford jewelry made entirely of gold or silver, while bronze and gold-plated bronze pieces were more cost-effective and worn by the common people. The Minoans were able to trade for or mine a variety of semi-precious stones and minerals that offered bright colors and contrasts. Favorites appeared to be lapis lazuli (blue), carnelian (orange), garnet (deep red), and obsidian (black). Sometimes jewelers would also use jasper, a stone which was available in a variety of hues, including the rare green. Amethysts came from Egypt and experienced a burst of popularity among the Minoans, partly because they were somewhat inexpensive to trade. According to several scholars, the decline in the value of the amethyst occurred once the Egyptian nobility stopped favoring the semi-precious stone. In short, the vibrant purple material fell out of fashion.[28]

---

[28] Jacke Phillips, "Egyptian Amethyst in the Bronze Age Aegean," *Journal of Ancient Egypt Interconnections* 1, no. 2 (2009).

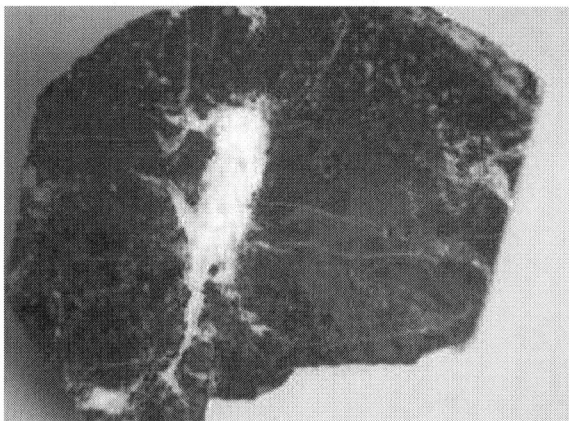

Amethyst and Lapis Lazuli

Other choices were more creative items and materials like shells, which could be gathered along the coasts of Thera and Crete. Steatite, or soapstone, was a hard mineral with a creamy, semi-translucent appearance that stood out against metal gathered from local islands. The Minoans traded for ivory from Africa as well. Blue materials continued to experience some of the highest demand due to the color's rarity in the natural world, as well as the Minoan's enjoyment of sea and water-based décor and motifs. Traders would sail to Egypt to bring back a substance called blue frit, or Egyptian blue, which was a synthetic material that was not quite Egyptian faience and not glass.

Egyptian faience, in general, proved to be fashionable. Egyptian faience was a particular substance developed by the Egyptians out of quartz and sand. The result was a glassy, moldable material that could be shaped, hardened, and dried. Finishes would be applied to the exterior so the end product would change to a new color once exposed to the heat of the drying process. These finishes included varying amounts of copper oxide, magnesium, calcium, potassium, and sodium. Again, the most popular choice of color for Egyptian faience was blue, although the Minoans also imported the material in green, red, black, and white. Some chemical analysis also indicates that the Minoans might have known how to make their own faience, potentially by mimicking methods learned from Egyptian craftsmen.[29] Again, the favored color was a bright blue that wasn't light but also not too rich. The best example of the color actually comes from an Egyptian artifact (and a personal favorite of this author), "William" the hippo.

"William," the Ancient Egyptian Faience Hippopotamus

Despite being the rarest commodity, gold was favored because it symbolized the wearer's status and wealth. Only those of high

[29] M.S. Tite; Y. Maniatis; D. Kavoussanaki; M. Panagiotakic; J. Shortland; S.F. Kirk, "Colour in Minoan faience," *Journal of Archaeological Science* 36, no. 2 (2009): pgs. 370-378.

economic status could afford even a single piece of gold jewelry. Gold is also a soft metal, making it easy to work with but also simple to scratch. Metalworkers would need the experience necessary not to ruin their supplies, and their craftsmanship showed in their finished products. Due to its softness, gold appeared in numerous forms in jewelry. It could be beaten, embossed, engraved, and even punched with stamps to make a consistent design. It could also be transformed into more delicate materials like filigree or gold leaf. Some jewelry even shows the old technique of granulation, where minuscule gold spheres could be attached to a main piece of jewelry by applying and heating a mixture of copper salt and glue to the desired connection. This gold work was not for the faint of heart.

The Minoans produced almost every type of jewelry imaginable, including necklaces, bracelets, diadems, hairpins, chains, brooches, armlets, and even pectoral pieces. However, rings bore some of the greatest cultural significance because they could be used as seals on administrative documents. These rings bore distinct carvings that would form a design when pressed into hot wax. Many seal rings were solid gold, although some also included shells and hard materials that wouldn't be affected by the wax. Some could be opened and closed to expose the seal. The standard design was a convex oval attached at a right angle to the hoop of the ring.

"The Ring of Minos," c. 1500 – 1400 BCE

Signet or seal rings bore all types of patterns and full miniature scenes of events with cultural significance, including bull-leaping and hunting. Landscapes and animals were frequently depicted, including insects and arachnids like butterflies and spiders.[30] Like much Minoan jewelry and art, the artists preferred to fill the entire surface with engravings so different elements fought for space. This makes the total image difficult to see in several cases but is also a testament to the craftsmanship of the workers. At present, archaeologists have discovered over two hundred separate rings or lasting impressions, demonstrating the prevalence and importance of the seal ring.

An enduring legacy of the Minoans was their jewelry. Their techniques and styles continued to be used by other Aegean communities long after their civilization disappeared. Their successors, the Mycenaeans and the ancient Greeks, continued to use gold, included subjects like wildlife and flowers, and emphasized the importance of seals and luxury items as status symbols.

---

[30] Examples and a further study of the rings' cultural significance can be found in: "Tree Tugging and Omphalos Hugging on Minoan Gold Rings." In: Archaeologies of Cult: Essays on Ritual and Cult in Crete in Honor of Geraldine C. Gesell (Hesperia Suppl. 42), edited by Anna Lucia D'Agata and Aleydis van der Moortel, pp. 43-49. Princeton: American School of Classical Studies at Athens 2009.

Chapter 8 – Architecture

The Minoans possessed a form of architecture that was simple yet stylish. The majority of buildings used flat tiled roofs and stood between two and three stories high, including homes in cities. The lower walls would be made of compressed stone and rubble with little mortar, while mudbrick was used on the upper levels. Mudbrick is a building material composed of air-dried bricks made of a mixture of sand, loam, water, mud, and binding materials like plant husks. They were easy to make and have existed in some form since 7000 BCE. The Minoans fired their mudbrick, which made each individual brick more durable. Building interiors featured floors of flagstone, plaster, or wood. Some poorer homes might have used tamped earth, but there is little remaining proof.

Important buildings like palaces and villas were built from sturdier, more difficult to obtain materials like limestone, sandstone, and gypsum. There was no single pattern for construction, as buildings in different locations relied on either heavy, megalithic blocks of material or ashlar masonry. Ashlar stones were carefully cut to be even, small, and stable. Palaces and regular buildings alike used ceiling timbers to keep the roof in place.

Because the island settlements were small, the Minoans could have paved their roads using spare stones. This facilitated the movement of ox-drawn carts between farms, the coast, and the cities.

Plumbing

People sometimes forget that while modern plumbing is a luxury ancient humans lacked, civilizations still built intricate systems designed to handle waste management. Especially around the Mediterranean Sea and farther east toward the Levant, societies constructed sewer systems and avoided the disgusting conditions of the medieval Europeans, whom many modern audiences tend to think of when trying to imagine historical plumbing.

For the Minoans, the most important aspect of plumbing was the development of large, extensive waterways that could provide fresh water and also carry away waste and undesirable stormwater that might be contaminated with filth.[31] The Minoans were advanced and created their own aqueducts, cisterns, and isolated wells to ensure that fresh water, a precious resource in the middle of the sea, did not go to waste or become mixed with human waste. To facilitate plumbing, construction workers included the building of architecture into their designs. For example, the Minoan penchant for flat roofs and sloping entrances into open courtyards helped individuals gather the water from the rain and place it in cisterns.[32] Large structures like palaces also tended to have pipes that ran through and around the building, chasing water into designated storage areas.

[31] J.B, Rose and A.N, Angelakis, *Evolution of Sanitation and Wastewater Technologies through the Centuries*. London: IWA Publishing, 2014, pg. 2.
[32] Rose and Angelakis, *Evolution of Sanitation*, pg. 5.

Knossos' Palace Sewers Featuring a Stone Pipe

Even more mind-blowing is that the Minoans developed some of the first water treatment devices. The most common was a porous clay pipe that water could flow through repeatedly. The water would slip through the pores in the clay, leaving behind dirt and debris too large to make it through the microscopic holes. As one can imagine, though, most examples of intricate plumbing came from the cities, and there is speculation that Minoans in rural areas were forced to live without. However, rural families still possessed the common sense to store rain and freshwater in separate cisterns or even pots to keep it clean and away from human and animal waste.

Palaces and Columns

Palaces were large building complexes designed to serve administrative and defensive purposes. Records and trading accounts could be stored in archives and kept safe from the environment, and people could also seek shelter behind the walls during attacks and natural disasters like the tsunami that hit Crete. The majority of palaces have been discovered by archaeologists on Crete, primarily in the city of Knossos. Each excavated palace possesses unique characteristics, but all Minoan palaces share some basic features like giant columns, courtyards, designated storage areas, multiple floors, and sturdy interior and exterior staircases. Because the palaces needed to survive multiple generations and preserve goods and records, they were constructed from heavy stone for maximum durability.

Archaeologists date the first palaces to the end of the Early Minoan period around the third millennium BCE. The oldest existing structures can be found at Malia and provide some basic information about the Minoan construction plan.[33] Due to the variations in foundation age for sections of the same structure, scholars believe the Minoans originally built smaller palaces and then added new developments over time to suit the needs of the community. Although there are some differences in the styles of the Early, Middle, and Late Minoan time periods, architecture and design did not change much over the centuries. Newer palaces from the Middle Minoans shared common traits with Early Minoan construction styles, including space for western courts and detailed western facades that included extra reinforcement and decoration. Some believe such treatment indicates that the cardinal direction west held some cultural significance.

[33] Donald Preziosi and Louise A. Hitchcock, *Aegean Art and Architecture*, Oxford History of Art series, Oxford University Press, 1999.

Stone Ruins of the Palace of Knossos

Palaces were built to match preexisting geographical features and topography for maximum stability and flow. The buildings also aligned with significant landmarks like Mount Ida and Mount Juktas on a distinctive north-south axis, indicating the mountains possessed a form of ritual significance.[34] An example of this type of behavior from more modern societies would be the tendency of Christian churches to face east toward the sun due to the importance of the sunrise. This trend seemed to become less important in palaces constructed during the late Middle Minoan period, although the west facades were still given special treatment through the use of sandstone ashlar masonry.

Despite numerous similarities, palace architecture did slowly change due to the implementation of more efficient building techniques and a population increase that made construction easier. For this reason, scholars tend to divide architecture into the First Palace Period and the Second Palace Period. During the First Palace Period, the interior construction of a palace followed a basic square room by square

---

[34] Ibid.

room design where individuals would enter and walk directly from one room to another without intermediary structures like corridors. By the Second Palace Period, this simplistic design fell out of favor and was replaced with the tendency to build more elaborate internal divisions, hallways, and "gap" areas between main rooms.

Much of the current information about Minoan palace structure comes from the largest and most complete Minoan ruin in existence: the palace of Knossos.[35] This palace measures roughly 492 ft. across and has an area of 215,278 sq. ft. Some speculate the upper floors of the structure possessed over one thousand separate chambers varying in size and separated by corridors. The palace was so extensive during its time that many associate it with the Greek myth of the bull of Minos, or the Minotaur, from which the Minoans get their modern name thanks to Arthur Evans.

An Existing Segment of the Palace of Knossos

The palace of Knossos features perhaps the greatest Minoan contribution to the architecture of the Mediterranean, which is the red columns seen in the photo above. These columns were inverted, which means the top is wider than the base. This style was the

---

[35] Anna Lucia D'Agata, "The Many Lives of a Ruin: History and Metahistory of the Palace of Minos at Knossos," *British School at Athens Studies* 18 (2010).

opposite of that used by the Greeks, who favored broader bases that accentuated the height of the structure. The Minoans additionally made their columns of wood rather than stone, although the column was mounted on a basic rock base for stability. The top of the columns tended to be rounded or pillowed, again drawing attention upward and putting emphasis on the ceiling.[36]

The architecture of the palace of Knossos is more complex than that of other existing sites, with the entire structure built around a central court and consisting of extensive porticos, stairways, chambers, storage areas, and a potential beautification room where men and women alike would go for makeup—some scholars even consider it to be the equivalent of a modern-day salon! Chambers on different levels might be connected by ramps, hidden staircases, or built into previously existing geographic features like hillsides, giving the entire palace an elaborate but haphazard appearance. Despite this, the palace of Knossos is beautiful, featuring some of the most detailed and colorful frescoes painted by the Minoans. These frescoes were not just reserved for the throne room, as they were even found in storage areas.

Palace Dolphin Fresco

Once again, the most common subjects of artwork were the ever-present dolphin, fish, flowers, saffron, and bull-leapers. Some areas,

---

[36] F. Bourbon, Lost *Civilizations*, New York: Barnes and Noble, Inc., 1998.

such as the throne room, feature more unusual creatures, including a lounging red animal with a decorative appearance. Red and blue were the most popular colors.

Chapter 9 – Theories about the Collapse of Civilization

By all accounts, the Minoans had a thriving civilization and appeared to have a hold on the sea surrounding their islands. These advantages did not save them, though, from eventually crumbling and losing their culture to their nearby neighbors like the Mycenaeans. Evidence gathered from islands like Crete indicate something enormous happened that pushed the Minoans out of their favorable situation, making them easy prey for more militaristic neighbors. At present, there is one major theory about why the Minoan civilization collapsed: the results of the Thera eruption.

The Minoan Eruption Theory

The Minoan home of Santorini existed in a dangerous location. As one can see in the accompanying image, the Santorini island group consisted of several small landmasses, including Santorini (Thera) itself, Therasia, and the Kameni Islands. At the center of this group was a caldera that still exists in contemporary times. A caldera is a cauldron-like hollow in a volcanic region that forms when a magma chamber or reservoir erupts. This sudden evacuation displaces the ground, resulting in a collapse that creates a sinkhole of soft earth and molten material. Over time, the caldera can slowly refill with magma from surrounding volcanic bodies and become ready for eruption once more.

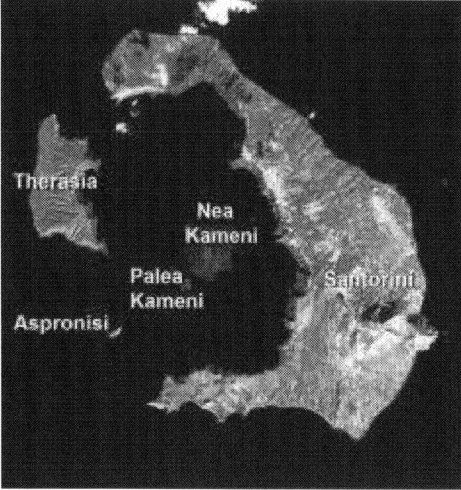

The Santorini Caldera

Today, the Santorini caldera measures 7.5 x 4.3 miles and has cliffs of 980 ft. on three sides. Overlapping shield volcanos form the basis of the caldera and often create new, smaller calderas from their eruptions. The two islands in the center, Nea Kameni and Palea Kameni, are made of volcanic rock and ash from previous eruptions.

The Greek archaeologist Spyridon Marinatos developed the Minoan eruption theory between 1935 and 1939. According to this theory, there was a massive eruption on Thera between 1550 and 1500 BCE. It was one of the largest volcanic explosions in known history and ejected between 14 and 24 cubic miles of material. On the modern scale of the Volcanic Explosivity Index, the eruption ranked a 7.[37]

---

[37] Sigurdsson H, Carey, S, Alexandri M, Vougioukalakis G, Croff K, Roman C, Sakellariou D, Anagnostou C, Rousakis G, Ioakim C, Gogou A, Ballas D, Misaridis T, & Nomikou P, "Marine Investigations of Greece's Santorini Volcanic Field," *Eos* 87, no. 34 (2006).

The Santorini eruption generated so much flow that it devastated the nearby Minoan settlement of Akrotiri and covered it in a thick layer of pumice. Santorini was roughly 62 miles from Crete, where the main Minoan settlements sat. According to Marinatos, the eruption was so devastating that it severely affected the development and stability of the Minoan culture. In theories from the first half of the 20th century, scholars proposed that so much volcanic ash came from the explosion on Thera that the plant life on the eastern half of Crete was completely choked and unable to grow. This starved the local population and prevented new growth and the further development of culture and military.

After closer examinations with modern instruments, scientists discovered that no more than 5 millimeters of ash covered any section of Crete, indicating that plant growth would not have been affected by volcanic material. Instead, there was evidence of something just as deadly. The explosion on Thera generated so much force that a massive tsunami hit the coast of Crete and destroyed the settlements along the eastern half of the island.[38] The town of Knossos lost most of its wealth and significance, and the regional importance of the settlement declined.

However, the decline was not immediate. Numerous remains have · been found in the 16th century Minoan Thera ash layer that indicate the collapse was not immediate. People continued to live, create art, reproduce, and trade with surrounding civilizations, but the eruption caused significant problems. Because the Minoans relied on their position as a sea power, the disruption of the tsunami threw a wrench into their operation. Evidence indicates many of their seafaring vessels would have been destroyed, and the storehouses and goods in Knossos and other settlements on the east coast of Crete would be gone as well. This meant trade and general defense declined significantly.

---

[38] Floyd W. McCoy and Grant Heiken, "Tsunami Generated by the Late Bronze Age Eruption of Thera (Santorini), Greece," *Pure and Applied Geophysics*, 157, no. 157 (2000).

Whether or not the destruction was enough to immediately initiate the collapse of the civilization is the subject of hot debate. The settlements on Crete show that Mycenaean weaponry was buried at the sites soon after the initial eruption, and the Mycenaeans still took several decades to depose the Minoans. What is certain is that the eruption resulted in a severe economic and resource crisis that made the Minoans vulnerable to attack. According to the scholar Sinclair Hood, the Minoans probably succumbed to an invading force following the eruption.[39] He and several others believe that, due to the unevenness of the damage and destruction on Crete, the Mycenaeans were the real destroyers of the Minoan civilization on Crete. This is further evidenced by the fact that the palace at Knossos was mostly preserved and used by the Mycenaeans later on. There was also severe deforestation in the area, meaning the Minoans managed to exceed the region's environmental capacity.[40] It's likely the Minoans were already on the verge of collapse before the eruption due to the stripping of resources.

The Atlantis Interpretation

The Atlantis interpretation of the Minoan fate takes much of its inspiration from the Thera eruption that devastated Santorini and potentially Crete. Because this eruption generated enough force to create a massive tsunami, some believe that the fate of the Minoans not only inspired the modern tale of Atlantis but actually happened. In many ways, the idea that the Minoan civilization became Atlantis is a conspiracy theory since there is no hard evidence for a secret underwater city. However, archaeologists and historians do believe the events that led to the Minoan collapse were responsible for the development of the Atlantean narrative.

Greek writers like Plato wrote extensively about a city that was enveloped by the sea and sank into the water but are vague about the

---

[39] Sinclair Hood, *The Minoans: Crete in the Bronze Age*, London: Thames & Hudson, 1971.
[40] J.D.S. Pendlebury and Arthur Evans, *Handbook to the Palace of Minos and Knossos with Its Dependencies*, Kessinger Publishing, 2003.

details. Some documents indicate it happened under the "Pillars of Hercules," mountains on the Gulf of Laconia, the southernmost gulf of ancient Greece. The settlement that was the inspiration for Atlantis was destroyed, but the rhetoric is vague about whether it actually disappeared entirely into the water or not. Most scholars think the language is just a form of creative license and that the Thera eruption, combined with the Late Bronze Age Collapse and the fall of the Minoans, was what the Greeks referred to when talking about Atlantis.[41]

L. Bakst, Terror Antiquus, 1908

Whether one subscribes to the conspiracy theory or sticks more to scholarly interpretations, it's clear that the Thera eruption was perhaps the most significant event to happen to the Minoans. They lost their culture, important settlements, and civilization due to a random natural disaster rather than any personal failing or wrongdoing.

---

[41] Spyridon Marinatos, *Some Words about the Legend at Atlantis* (2nd ed.), Athens: C. Papachrysanthou, 1972.

Conclusion – Where Are They Now?

When discussing ancient civilizations, there almost always is one question prevalent in contemporary minds: What happened to them? While this query can be related to mysterious disappearances, there is also another fundamental reason for the question: Often, individuals want to know if the ancient civilization could be their predecessors or ancestors. Modern professionals in the fields of archaeogenetics have spent the last decade working to discover where the Minoans went through the examination of genetic material pulled from ancient skeletons. These professionals can compare the information taken from mtDNA to determine whether the Minoans were absorbed into the Mycenaean civilization and eventually the Greeks, if they moved to a new location and reproduced with an existing group of peoples (thus changing the general traits recorded in DNA), or if they instead were wiped out through a combination of warfare and natural disasters.

While the studies of archaeogeneticists can answer burning personal questions, they can also provide a clue to other professionals about the movement of different groups of people.[42] The field of genetics, when applied to history, has demonstrated that most groups of humans are the descendants of a few specific individuals who carried separate genetic traits. This information is important in determining how different ethnic groups developed with specific genes and adaptations. While the mtDNA taken from the Minoans doesn't say much about distinct traits, it does allow archaeologists to answer the question: Where are they now?

In 2013, a group of archaeogeneticists took mtDNA from a sample of ancient Minoan skeletons that were found sealed in a cave in the Lasithi Plateau. What happened to the individuals is unknown, but the preserved bones date back between 3,700 and 4,400 years.[43] The team compared the Minoan mtDNA to samples taken from native residents of Greece, Egypt, general North Africa, Anatolia, and a broad spectrum of places across western and northern Europe. The results of the study indicated that the Minoans shared similar genetics with modern Cretans and Neolithic Europeans to the north and west. There were few to no similarities with Egyptian or Libyan populations, which means the Minoans did not move south into Africa after their civilization collapsed. This evidence does support the idea that the Minoans were absorbed into populations to the north and that their successors most likely did not leave the island of Crete. According to the study's co-author, George Stamatoyannopoulos from the University of Washington, "We now know that the founders of the first advanced European civilization were European. They were very similar to Neolithic Europeans and very similar to present day-Cretans."[44]

In 2017, another archaeogenetics study was completed on a separate group of Minoan remains. This work concluded that the Minoans

---

[42] A. Bouwman and F. Rühli, "Archaeogenetics in Evolutionary Medicine," *Journal of Molecular Medicine* 94 (2016): pgs. 971-977. doi: 10.1007/s00109-016-1438-8
[43] Hughey, Jeffrey. "A European Population in Minoan Bronze Age Crete." *Nature Communications* 4 (2013): pg. 1861. 10.1038/ncomms2871.
[44] Tia Ghose, "Mysterious Minoans Were European, DNA Finds," *LiveScience*, 2013.

were genetically related to the Mycenaean Greeks and had similar but not identical traits. The DNA was then compared to modern Greek populations. Based on the results, scholars could conclude that the Minoans, Mycenaeans, and ancient Greeks were all related and that the same genetic strains continued into contemporary times. In short, the Minoans live on in the modern Greek population and others who hail from the Mediterranean on the European side.[45]

It can be difficult for people to understand why ancient civilizations are important to the modern world, especially when discussing a group as small as the Minoans. However, the Minoans paved the way for peoples like the Mycenaeans, who would then influence the culture of the ancient Greeks, who continue to be one of the most enduring European peoples in the world. From a social aspect, learning about the Minoans can demonstrate that the ancient world was not a solid mass. Reading about the oldest civilizations can often make people believe that humans developed in one way—heavy agriculture, strict gender roles, feudal societies, and massive armies. The Minoans defied these standards by offering a civilization based on commerce with almost equal rights for men and women, room for social advancement, and a navy that spent most of its time trading.

Without the Minoans, modern life wouldn't be the same at all.

---

[45] Brigit Katz, "DNA Analysis Sheds Light on the Mysterious Origins of the Ancient Greeks," *Smithsonian.*

Check out another book by Captivating History

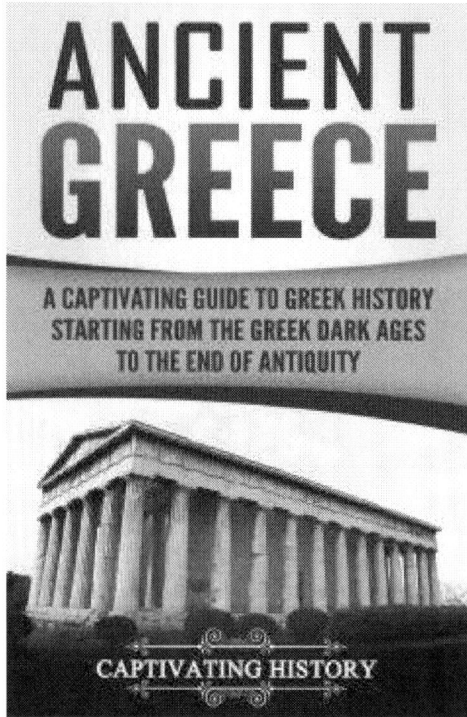

Bibliography

Adams, Ellen. *Cultural Identity in Minoan Crete: Social Dynamics in the Neopalatial Period.* New York: Cambridge University Press, 2017.

Betancourt, Philip B. *The History of Minoan Pottery.* Princeton: Princeton University Press, 1985.

Bourbon, F. *Lost Civilizations.* Barnes and Noble, Inc. New York, 1998.

Bouwman A. and Rühli, F. "Archaeogenetics in Evolutionary Medicine." *Journal of Molecular Medicine* 94 (2016): pgs. 971-977. 10.1007/s00109-016-1438-8

Cameron, M.A.S.; Jones R. E. and Philippakis, S.E. "Scientific Analyses of Minoan Fresco Samples from Knossos." *The Annual of the British School at Athens* 72 (1977): pgs. 121-184.

Carr, H. Graham. "Some Dental Characteristics of the Minoans." *Royal Anthropological Institute of Great Britain and Ireland* 60 (August 1960): pg. 119-122. https://www.jstor.org/stable/2797174.

Castleden, Rodney. *Minoans: Life in Bronze Age Crete.* New York: Routledge, 1993.

Cole, Sara. "The Wall Paintings of Tell el-Dab'a: Potential Aegean Connections." Pursuit - *The Journal of Undergraduate Research at the University of Tennessee* 1, no. 1 (2010).

D'Agata, Anna Lucia. "The Many Lives of a Ruin: History and Metahistory of the Palace of Minos at Knossos." *British School at Athens Studies* 18 (2010).

Gillis, Carole and Nosch, Marie-Louise B. *Ancient Textiles: Production, Crafts and Society.* Oxford: Oxbow Books, 2007.

Ghose, Tia. "Mysterious Minoans Were European, DNA Finds." *LiveScience.* 2013.

Higgins, Reynold. *Minoan and Mycenaean Art.* London: Thames and Hudson, 1997.

Higgins, R. *The Aegina Treasure - An Archaeological Mystery.* London: 1979.

Hood, Sinclair. *The Minoans: Crete in the Bronze Age.* London: Thames & Hudson, 1971.

Hughey, Jeffrey. "A European Population in Minoan Bronze Age Crete." *Nature Communications* 4 (2013): pg. 1861. 10.1038/ncomms2871.

J.S. "Saffron and the Minoans." *Pharmacy in History* 47, no. 1 (2005): pg. 28-31. https://www.jstor.org/stable/41112251.

Jones, Bernice R. "Revealing Minoan Fashions." *Archaeology* 53, no. 3 (May/June 2000): pg. 36-41. https://www.jstor.org/stable/41779314.

Katz, Brigit. "DNA Analysis Sheds Light on the Mysterious Origins of the Ancient Greeks." *Smithsonian.*

Lobell, Jarrett A. "The Minoans of Crete." *Archaeology* 68, no. 3 (May/June 2015): pg. 28-35. https://www.jstor.org/stable/24364735.

Manning, Sturt W.; Ramsey, Christopher Bronk; Kutschera, Walter; Higham, Thomas; Kromer, Bernd; Steier, Peter; and Wild, Eva M. "Chronology for the Aegean Late Bronze Age 1700-1400 B.C." *Science* 28, no. 312 (2006): pg. 565-569. 10.1126/science.1125682.

Marinatos, Nanno. "Minoan Religion." Columbia: University of South Carolina.

Marinatos, Spyridon. *Some Words about the Legend at Atlantis* (2nd ed.). Athens: C. Papachrysanthou, 1972.

McCoy, Floyd W. and Heiken, Grant. "Tsunami Generated by the Late Bronze Age Eruption of Thera (Santorini), Greece." *Pure and Applied Geophysics* 157, no 157 (2000).

McEnro, John C. *Architecture of Minoan Crete: Constructing Identity in the Aegean Bronze Age.* University of Texas Press, 2010.

Molloy, Barry P.C. "Martial Minoans? War as Social Process, Practice and Event in Bronze Age Crete." *The Annual of the British School at Athens* 107 (2012): pg. 87-142. https://www.jstor.org/stable/41721880.

Noble, J.V. "The Wax of the Lost Wax Process". *American Journal of Archaeology.* 79, no. 4 (1975).

Pendlebury J.D.S. and Evans, Arthur. *Handbook to the Palace of Minos and Knossos with Its Dependencies.* Kessinger Publishing, 2003.

Phillips, Jacke. "Egyptian Amethyst in the Bronze Age Aegean." *Journal of Ancient Egypt Interconnections* 1, no. 2 (2009). DOI:10.2458/azu_jaei_v01i2_phillips.

Preziosi, Donald & Hitchcock, Louise A. *Aegean Art and Architecture*. Oxford History of Art series, Oxford University Press, 1999.

Pulak, Cemal and Bass, George F. "Bronze Age Shipwreck Excavation at Uluburun." Institute of Nautical Archaeology.

Rose J.B. and Angelakis, A.N. *Evolution of Sanitation and Wastewater Technologies through the Centuries*. London: IWA Publishing, 2014.

Schofield, Louise. *The Mycenaeans*. J. Paul Getty Museum, 2007.

Sigurdsson H, Carey, S, Alexandri M, Vougioukalakis G, Croff K, Roman C, Sakellariou D, Anagnostou C, Rousakis G, Ioakim C, Gogou A, Ballas D, Misaridis T, & Nomikou P. "Marine Investigations of Greece's Santorini Volcanic Field." *Eos* 87, no. 3 (2010).

Thompson, James G. "Clues to the Location of Bull Jumping at Zakros." *Journal of Sport History* 19, no. 2 (1992): pg. 163-168. https://www.jstor.org/stable/43610538.

Tite, M.S.; Y. Maniatis; D. Kavoussanaki; M. Panagiotakic; J. Shortland; S.F. Kirk. "Colour in Minoan faience." *Journal of Archaeological Science* 36, no. 2 (2009): pgs. 370-378.

Warren, Peter. "Knossos: New Excavations and Discoveries." *Archaeology* (July /August 1984): p. 48-55.

Weiner, Malcolm. "Realities of Power: The Minoan Thalassocracy in Historical Perspective." *AMILLA: The Quest for Excellence*, 2013. doi: http://www.academia.edu/30141237/_Realities_of_Power_T he_Minoan_Thalassocracy_in_Historical_Perspective_AMIL LA_The_Quest_for_Excellence._Studies_Presented_to_Gue nter_Kopcke_in_Celebration_of_His_75th_Birthday_2013_p p._149_173